D1077837

Seen and heard

Involving disabled children and young people in research and development projects

Linda Ward

In memory of

Alison Blake

Greater Manchester Coalition of Disabled People
Young Disabled People's Project

The **Joseph Rowntree Foundation** has supported this project as part of its programme of research and innovative development projects, which it hopes will be of value to policy makers and practitioners. The facts presented and views expressed in this report are, however, those of the author and not necessarily those of the Foundation.

Published by YPS for the Joseph Rowntree Foundation

ISBN 1 899987 48 7

Illustrations by Angela Martin

Prepared and printed by:
York Publishing Services Ltd
64 Hallfield Road
Layerthorpe
York YO3 7XQ

Contents

Acknowledgements

Thanks to the many people who strengthened this through their helpful comments, especially Barbara Ballard, Bryony Beresford, Karen Clarke, Barbara Fletcher, Margaret Flynn, Caroline Glendinning, Gerison Lansdown, Janet Lewis, Lesley Jones, Ruth Marchant, Roger Mattingly, Jenny Morris, Maureen Oswin, Terry Philpot, Helen Roberts, Philippa Russell, Robina Shah, Ruth Sinclair, Tricia Sloper and Derek Williams.

Introduction

Consulting children and involving people who use services in their planning and development have been key developments of the last decade, officially encouraged by the Children Act 1989 and the NHS and Community Care Act 1990. This concern to involve and empower service users in the projects and developments which affect their lives has been shared and actively promoted by the Joseph Rowntree Foundation.

Now, the Foundation has embarked on a substantial research and development programme on issues concerning disabled children and young people and their families, as part of its wider Social Care and Disability Programme. A central feature of that programme has been a commitment to the involvement of service users in projects supported by the Foundation, not just as 'subjects' or beneficiaries of projects but as partners, consultants, advisers, interviewers and so on. The idea has been that disabled adults should, so far as possible, be involved in every stage of the project process. We believe this to be right, and that where it is done well, it enhances the quality and relevance of projects undertaken. This principle is now being extended to our new initiative. Our expectation is that disabled children and young adults will be active participants in all projects concerning them, though we recognise that the involvement of some children (those with profound and multiple impairments who may not communicate through speech or conventional signs) may pose particular challenges. Involving children rather than adults entails additional ethical and practical issues; careful attention must be paid to safeguards and strategies for their well-being.

This paper identifies key issues of concern and summarises some existing work which addresses them. It outlines some strategies and provides a checklist for consideration by those wishing to undertake work in this area.

Experience in listening to and involving children and young people in research and development projects is relatively new in the UK. For disabled children and young people it is rare, so this paper is only a starting point. New ways of involving disabled children appropriately in projects affecting them are emerging. Experience gained through projects funded under the programme will be actively shared with the wider academic, research and practitioner communities, as well as with disabled children and young people themselves (and their families and organisations representing them) in order to develop an accumulation of expertise in involving disabled children and young people in projects that affect their lives. In the meantime, we believe that the ideas set out here will be of interest to a wider audience.

In future, all proposals submitted to the Foundation for funding within this programme will be expected to show careful consideration of how the issues outlined here will be addressed within each particular project. Projects which are successful in gaining funding will be expected to pay continuing attention to ethical issues and safeguards for participating children throughout the different stages of the project's development.

1 Involving children and young people: background, context and the law

Children do not acquire full autonomy to exercise freedom of choice in all areas that affect their lives until they are 18. However, over recent decades there have been changes in their status and growing recognition that they are individuals separate from, as well as part of, their families. The key developments in this area are described in this chapter.

The UN Convention on the Rights of the Child

This was adopted by the United Nations General Assembly in 1989 and ratified by the UK Government in December 1991. Article 12 is particularly relevant:

> State Parties shall assure to the child who is capable of forming his or her own views the right to express those views freely in all matters affecting the child, the views of the child being given due weight in accordance with the age and maturity of the child.

This means that in the UK we recognise in principle the child's right to express an opinion and to have that opinion taken into account in any matter affecting them.

The Gillick judgement

Most case law on children's consent focuses on decisions about medical treatment or residence. Children who are judged to be 'competent' have certain rights with regard to consent. Legal views on competence to consent hinge less on the child's chronological age than on their ability or competence (Alderson, 1995).

The Gillick case in the 1980s led to a House of Lords ruling on how far a parent has authority in relation to decision-making on behalf of their child. The ruling asserts that children who are competent to make a decision affecting their lives are entitled to do so. Parental power is transferred to competent children, not shared with them (Alderson, 1995). This ruling has not, however, been incorporated into primary legislation; in practice, assessment of competence can be problematic and, where there is disagreement, judges may well support the views of adults rather than children.

The situation has been muddied further by subsequent rulings in the Court of Appeal (see Alderson, 1995, pp. 72–5). In the 1992 *in re* W case, the judges ruled that young people aged under 18 years have no absolute right to make their own decisions on medical treatment (see Alderson, 1995, pp. 73 and 74 for further details). This ruling undermines the statement within the Children Act (see page 5) that children can refuse court-recommended medical and psychiatric examination and that courts should take

account of children's views. There was criticism of the ruling for its denial of young people's rights to consent and refusal. Alderson points out that similar cases are being heard elsewhere which may be going unreported. Some judges may be making more liberal rulings, but the reported cases influence subsequent ones (Alderson, 1995).

The Children Act 1989

The Gillick ruling paved the way for children to have the right to be consulted about all decisions which affect them: medical treatment, residence and contact with their parents, education, religion and welfare (Alderson, 1995). The ruling was echoed in the Children Act 1989 which embodies a number of key principles that demonstrate respect for the views of children (Lansdown, 1995). The significance of their race, religion, language and culture are also addressed for the first time. The Act requires local authorities and courts to consider the wishes and feelings of children when making decisions concerning their welfare. Children who are subject to a Child Assessment Order, for example, and who are competent to make informed choices can refuse to be examined under the Act. Partly as a result of the Act, some authorities are exploring methods of encouraging children to participate both in decision-making affecting their own lives and in the development of policies which may affect them more generally. The Children (Scotland) Act 1995 introduces a much broader principle of the right of children to be consulted on matters of concern to them (Lansdown, 1995).

Other initiatives

The desirability of getting children involved in matters that affect them has also been shown in various other developments in different areas. In the health service, for example, an initiative by the Royal College of Nursing provided awards to innovative developments which promoted children's participation in their own health care, and the Patient's Charter on Services for Children and Young People acknowledged children and young people's rights with regard to access to records and involvement in decision-making about health care treatment and prevention measures (Department of Health, 1996).

In the field of education, the Code of Practice on Special Educational Needs (Department for Education, 1994) states:

> Schools should ... make every effort to identify the ascertainable views and wishes of the child about his or her current and future education.

The role of the 'named person' – a person chosen by the local education authority to give information about a child's special educational needs – may be particularly significant here in relation to consultations with children from black and ethnic minority groups and their families. The named person may be someone known to, and chosen by, the child or their family to articulate and represent their needs and views on educational issues. This is clearly especially important where English is not the child or family's first language, and the named person can communicate both with them and the relevant professionals or authorities (Shah, 1995).

Russell (1996) gives a useful review of issues relating to listening and responding to children and young people in the light of both the Children Act 1993 and the Code of Practice.

Consent and competence

Involving children and young people in research and development projects requires keen attention to issues of consent and competence, issues which are returned to in Chapter 3 and explored in detail in Alderson (1995).

Research, ethics and empowerment

Within the field of social research generally, there has been a gradual shift over the last two decades towards a recognition of research as a social process in which researchers can do more or less to redress the balance of power between them and those they interview. The debate about developing more democratic research methods has been enhanced by the contribution of feminist researchers (see, for example, Helen Roberts, 1991, and Ann Oakley, 1991). In the 1990s disability research has come under close scrutiny and new frameworks for more 'emancipatory' or empowering

research have been put forward (Oliver, 1992). The Foundation-funded series of workshops in 1991–2 on 'Researching physical disability' inspired diverse contributions on different aspects of undertaking disability research in a more positive and less discriminatory way than has been traditional (see *Disability, Handicap and Society*, 1992). The whole subject of disability, research and empowerment has begun to receive attention which is long overdue (Ward and Flynn, 1994). There is now a small, but developing, literature on research with disabled children (see, for example, Alderson, 1995, and Beresford, 1997). Those embarking on projects involving disabled children and young people will do well to draw on the ideas put forward by experienced researchers with non-disabled children (see, for example, the special issue of *Children and Society*, 1996, which focused on the ethics and methodology of research with children), the insights deriving from recent disability research such as those cited above, and the important work by Marchant and Page in communicating with children with multiple impairments and those who do not speak (1993, 1997).

2 Involving children and young people as partners in projects

Promoting participation by disabled children and young people in research and development projects which may affect their lives means more than just involving them as the 'subjects' of research. It means discovering different ways in which they can be potentially involved throughout the lifetime of a project, from its early planning stages through to the sharing of its findings.

Planning

Sarah McCrum and Paul Bernal (1994), in a pamphlet aimed particularly at journalists, stress the value of consulting children when planning research for articles or programmes:

> You could try to find out what issues are particularly important from their perspective (often surprising), what kind of children might take part or be interviewed, where you can find the right children etc. These are all the same areas you would research for any interview but journalists often only ask adults, even when the subject concerns children.

They add:

> It is important to remember that children, like adults, talk best about subjects they are interested in – you will need to balance your agenda with theirs.

In some places groups of disabled young people will already exist and those seeking funding for projects from the Foundation will need to show that they have consulted with them to check that the work proposed addresses issues of concern to them or has been suggested by them or that the research or project is being carried out in partnership. Partnerships may be very productive: the group of disabled young people may know the important issues to address and are likely to have relevant insights and contacts. The other parties to the partnership may bring useful research skills to the joint process.

Projects conceived and run by disabled young people themselves are particularly welcome. The Foundation may suggest that a development project that is to be undertaken by a young disabled people's group might usefully be documented by another organisation so that lessons can be shared with others elsewhere, or suggest ways in which specialised advice and support (for example on research techniques) can be built in from other sources, if that seems appropriate or helpful.

Participation in the planning of projects makes it more likely that subsequent involvement of children and young people will be positive. Experience at The Who Cares? Trust suggests that where young people complain of bad experiences of involvement it often centres on 'not knowing what's going on' (Barbara Fletcher, personal communication). Involvement at the planning stage should avoid this and make it more likely that participating children and young people are given clear information on their role in the project and proper preparation and training as appropriate.

Consultancy

Disabled children and young people will inevitably have insights and perspectives which may differ sharply from those of adults undertaking projects within the Foundation's programme. In order to benefit from this expertise, projects might consider employing disabled young people as consultants to advise on different topics as the project progresses. As a general rule the Foundation would assume that some payment for this help would be made, as it would for adult consultants. Rates and methods of payment should be considered carefully. The Who Cares? Trust has developed experience in this area, as have other disabled people's and young people's organisations. In some situations, certificates or awards may be appropriate and well received by the young people involved as something to mark their participation which they can then keep.

Where it is not felt appropriate to involve disabled children or teenagers directly as consultants or advisers to a project, the contribution and insights of young disabled adults who are slightly older (say in their twenties) but have relevant experience and expertise will be valuable.

It is important to ensure that children and young people from a variety of backgrounds are consulted. Established voluntary organisations may not have many black and ethnic minority families in their membership, for example, but the local race equality council, council for voluntary service or local authority (particularly the race or equal opportunities adviser) should have information on relevant groups in the area.

A high proportion of disabled children from black and ethnic minority groups will be in special schools. They may provide a useful access point. You may well need to go through the children's parents in order to make contact with them. Although

you may want to keep your dealings with the children separate
from contact with their parents, visits with parents are likely to
serve a useful purpose in establishing trust and empowering them
to articulate their needs and views. This, in turn, may well
encourage the parents to agree to or facilitate their child's
Involvement. Consultancy with black and ethnic minority children
and their parents may mean working with an interpreter (see
Chapter 4 for more information about this).

Advisory groups

The Foundation likes to establish advisory groups to support the projects which it funds. These groups are made up of half a dozen or more people from a variety of backgrounds representing different interests relevant to the project (for example, someone from the social services department, from a health trust, a teacher, a parent, etc.). Where projects relate to disabled adults, the assumption is that some disabled adults will automatically be a part of the group. In the case of advisory groups for projects concerned with disabled children, it may be felt that young people might not find a group comprised largely of adults and professionals a positive experience. A separate consultative group of disabled young people focusing on aspects of the project of interest and concern to them is likely to be more appropriate. Children and young people in the group may well feel freer to comment than they would if their views were sought as individuals. (Though sometimes where the project topic is particularly personal, individual consultation may be preferred. Project workers need to be sensitive to both possibilities.)

Careful attention will need to be paid to appropriate times, venues, transport and other arrangements for group meetings. (Morris, 1996, has useful checklists for involving service users in meetings, much of which will be relevant in the organisation of meetings of disabled children and young people.) Again, payment of some kind may be appropriate. Some of the advantages of working with groups can be found in the literature on group interviews, and some of the strategies for making these work well are also relevant to the successful operation of advisory groups (see, for example, McCrum and Bernal, 1994; Alderson, 1995; Mahon *et al.*, 1996; Beresford, 1997).

Rosemary Tozer and Patricia Thornton (1995) give a useful account of their experience of establishing a reference group of older people to act as advisers to a research project. It may provide helpful ideas for those setting up groups of young people for a similar purpose, including strategies for creating positive links between a project advisory group made up of professionals and a consultative or reference group made up of non-professionals, like children or young people.

Interviewing, research and project work

There is now a growing awareness in the social research field of some of the benefits that may accrue when employing women in research on women's issues, people from black and minority ethnic groups on research on areas of concern to them, and disabled researchers on disability projects, though clearly non-disabled researchers with appropriate skills and experience (particularly those working in consultation or partnership with disabled people and their organisations) also have an important role to play.

The idea of involving young people as interviewers in projects is still, however, relatively novel. Alderson's report (1995) contains a useful account of Barnardo's Young Interviewers Project and includes copies of materials used within the project together with a report on the young interviewers' experiences and views. Overall, the project was successful; it was felt that in some cases the young people were able to operate more effectively with the special school interviewees because of their understanding of some of their circumstances. Although uncertain about their abilities to undertake the work beforehand, they were subsequently confident enough to suggest that in the future young people should be involved in the interviewer training process.

Analysis and production of material

Young people may also have a valuable contribution to make in planning and participating in the analysis of project findings and in the final stages of a project where material is being put together. Sarah McCrum and Paul Bernal (1994) stress the value of letting children have some say in these processes, perhaps looking at early drafts and making comments or even a fuller involvement. They point out that it is all too easy, once writing and editing is underway, to fall into a very 'adult' way of thinking:

Sometimes this is appropriate, but if you are trying to represent children's views it helps if you check as much as possible with children.

They quote one of the children involved in their project as saying:

If we couldn't have edited it, it would have been a whole different story and we couldn't have got our message across.

Clearly, where the disabled children or young people concerned cannot easily read then alternative means of sharing this process with them (via a group meeting and/or using audio or videotapes) will need to be followed.

Dissemination

The Foundation sets enormous importance on the dissemination of findings from its research and development projects both to policy makers and decision makers and also to those whom the research or development project may affect. Disabled young people will have a useful role to play in suggesting what the key messages from a project are for other disabled children and young people and how these messages can best be got across. They can advise not only on content but on the best format or medium. They may help with illustrations or by contributing to audiotape summaries of key points from the project.

Special schools may provide a useful access point for consulting disabled children and young people about appropriate dissemination strategies. They can also be a useful avenue for disseminating a project's key messages or findings once these have been finalised, along with mainstream schools and other relevant community organisations and services.

The Foundation is already supporting *Plain Facts*: accessible summaries of key messages from projects aimed at people with learning difficulties (Townsley and Gyde, 1997a). Guidance on how to produce information in this way is now available (Townsley and Gyde, 1997b). Accessible summaries in illustrated leaflets, cartoon form or on audio or videotape may be useful ways of disseminating project findings in which young people can play a prominent part.

Some disabled young people will also have an important role to play as contributors to conferences or workshops publicising a project's findings, as the three young interviewers involved in a study of disabled young people in further education (Ash *et al.*, 1996) did at the launch of Priscilla Alderson's book.

Involvement in the production of publications, in workshops or in other kinds of media work may well require skills training for the young people concerned. The Who Cares? Trust has a brief Code of Practice for journalists and young people giving useful advice for both parties in this area (The Who Cares? Trust, 1993). The ethnic minority press, radio stations and cable television are all useful channels for disseminating key messages from projects to black and ethnic minority disabled children and young people and their families.

In seeking the involvement of disabled children and young people as partners in research and development projects, it is important to try to involve children of different ages, genders, backgrounds, ethnic minority groups and with different impairments in order to build a range of perspectives into the project. (Chapter 4 has more ideas on how to go about this.)

3 Ethical projects with disabled children and young people

Ethical issues

Ethical standards in research have been developed more actively, historically, in relation to medical than social research. Alderson (1995) provides a helpful overview of the key themes in developments in this area. She points out that ethics do not provide clear, agreed solutions but are a means for exploring dilemmas. Since ethics are based on centuries of patriarchal law and philosophy, and older ideas about rights and duties discriminate against women and children, new ways of thinking for ethical research with children have to be developed. Traditional ethics have carried a strong theme of avoiding deliberate harm and therefore stressing the importance of non-interference. Alderson points out that the alternative harms, of protecting children so much that they are silenced and excluded from research, tend to be ignored.

Safeguards are important!

Within its Research and Development Programme, the Joseph Rowntree Foundation has always striven to ensure that the work it supports is conducted according to high ethical standards. Within its Social Care and Disability Programme, a strong emphasis has been placed on the views and wishes of disabled people and service users. The assumption within its Disabled Children and Young People's Programme is that only research and development projects which place disabled children and young people centre stage and which treat them, so far as is possible and appropriate, as partners within the project process, should be funded. Proper attention to strategies and safeguards for involving disabled children and young people in projects concerning them are seen to be of the highest importance.

Within medical research, there is a strong tradition of research ethics committees: committees to which medical researchers have to submit their proposals for vetting before they can proceed. There can be many problems with research ethics committees (Alderson, 1995); Blackburn (1994), for example, points out that there were no disabled people on the 23 separate research ethics committees to which she had to submit a multi-centred piece of disability research in which she was involved. But such committees perform a useful function in forcing researchers to think through at least some of the ethical issues posed by their projects.

Social research ethics committees are not common, but some system for ensuring that the ethical issues posed by social research (and development) projects are considered is important. It is assumed that any proposals submitted for funding under the Foundation's Disabled Children and Young People's Programme will explicitly draw attention to these issues and how they will be addressed. This should include detailed consideration of any kind of potential 'impact on children' of the research proposal through practical procedures for ensuring confidentiality, safe storage of information and so on (see Alderson, 1995, especially Sections 2, 3 and 5). Vetting procedures for researchers who will have significant unsupervised access to children need careful attention. Police checks may be desirable (though not always easy to achieve in practice). The Foundation's expectation is that disabled children and young people should be included wherever possible as active participants within research and development projects that affect them; the challenge is for researchers to develop strategies and safeguards to facilitate this happening appropriately.

Morrow and Richards (1996) provide a useful and detailed overview of the ethics of social research with children, including issues concerning vulnerability and competence and suggestions for ways forward.

Consent

Ethical research with disabled children and young people demands their informed consent to participation. (Some indication of key legislation in this area is given in Chapter 1.) Alderson (1995) reviews the whole area of consent to research with children in some detail. She points out that the House of Lords ruling on the Gillick judgement says that children under 16 can give legally effective consent to medical treatment; here, parental power is transferred to competent children, not just shared with them. However, Alderson points out that the law over consent to treatment and research concerning children remains very uncertain, the more so with regard to research since it is less easy to claim that it will be of direct intended benefit to the child concerned. A key issue is competence: whether the child is competent or incompetent and therefore can or cannot be appropriately involved in making decisions about whether to take part in research. Competence is categorised by Alderson as having three characteristics: understanding (being able to understand the relevant information); wisdom (being able to make a wise decision in the child's best interest); freedom/autonomy (being able to make a voluntary, uncoerced decision).

Competence is usually assessed by checking whether the child is able to make informed, wise and voluntary decisions. Here it is important to assess whether the researchers have provided enough clear, relevant information, helped children to make wise choices, respected their wisdom and not exerted pressure or used undue persuasion. Assessing competence can be complex and the assessors' own beliefs play a key part. Alderson reviews the reasons why children are not always judged to be competent, but argues persuasively that features of children's responses to research questions (for example, the inclusion of feelings, memory and imagination) can be understood as sources of great insight rather than as distortions of objectivity. (See also Beresford, 1997, on issues of ethics and consent.)

There is now a growing literature on the practicalities of gaining proper consent from children and young people to participate in research projects. For example, in a study of the impact of the Child Support Act, parents were not asked for consent to interview children but were asked only for their consent to make contact with the child (Mahon *et al.*, 1996). A separate approach was then made to the children at which their consent was sought; each child was asked again at the start of the interview whether they were willing to take part. Clearly, seeking consent from a parent to approach a child to see whether they wish to participate in a project may in practice have the same outcome as seeking the parent's consent for the child's participation: a parent not wishing their child to be involved may refuse to allow the researcher any contact in the first place. But at least seeking the child's consent separately from the parent does ensure that the child's chance to refuse or consent to involvement is maximised.

Cavet (1995) reviews practices as regards obtaining children's consent. She found that some researchers obtained written consent from both parents and their child before telephoning to organise interviews, while others obtained written permission from parents and children after arriving to carry out interviews. Many disabled children and young people (like many adults) will want strong reassurance that their views will not be passed on to services or other people with whom they are involved.

Be alert to non verbal signs!

Most researchers emphasise the importance of continuing to check with child respondents that they are willing to continue with interviews as they progress, and of the need to be alert to non-verbal signs, like body language, which indicate that they might wish to withdraw consent at any stage. Ruth Marchant (personal communication) stresses that researchers need to give children ways to initiate breaks, ask for explanations, refuse to answer certain questions and close the interaction. For many children it will help if they can practise this beforehand, for example: 'How would you let me know if you had had enough? How could I tell? Can you show me? Let's pretend that you want to stop.' This will be especially important for children who do not speak. Disabled children may be particularly used to having to do as adults (or professionals) tell them. They may need additional reassurance that the researcher will not be cross or upset if they want to end the session. Even where children wish to participate in a project, be alert to the possibility that they may decide at a later stage, or part-way through an interview, that they have changed their mind.

Some black and ethnic minority children and their families are more expressive in a mother tongue other than English; they will need the option of communicating in it. (For more details on involving children from black and ethnic minority groups, see Chapter 4.)

Consulting children with limited means of conventional communication poses additional problems with regard to gaining explicit consent. In Minkes *et al.*'s study (1994), parents' consent was sought on behalf of their children. Reasons for the apparently low rate of parental consent are discussed in their article. A significant number of disabled children and young people live, or spend much of their lives, away from their family homes. Negotiating access to such children in order to discover whether they wish to participate in projects will demand particularly careful attention. Alderson and Goodey (1996) give an open and illuminating account of the ethical and other issues that arose for them around access, consent and methodology in their research with disabled children and the strategies they adopted to deal with them.

Imaginative strategies for encouraging children and young people to think about whether or not they wish to participate in research are being developed. Section 12 of Alderson's report contains examples of information aimed at helping young people decide whether they wish to participate in researc projects and the questions that they might wish to ask the researchers involved. Researchers will need to build time into their projects if they are to work imaginatively in this area.

Putting an ethical approach into practice

Ideas and experience about how to improve the quality of research and development work with disabled children and young people are evolving constantly. Key issues and stages of the process are indicated below, together with references to where further information can be found. Clearly, disabled children and young people vary enormously in their abilities, interests, ways of communication and backgrounds, and each stage of the process of involvement will need to be tailored and adapted to individual needs.

Information leaflets

Simple leaflets, properly produced, should help children and young people understand better what participation in a particular project will entail and whether or not they wish to be involved. Alderson (1995, Section 2) gives useful information on the style and format leaflets should follow, including short lines, short words, requests rather than commands and so on. The design and content of leaflets need to be tailored to the different ages, abilities and circumstances of the particular group of young people concerned. The style and format of leaflets (for example, whether or not they include Makaton, signs, illustrations, large print and/or are available in languages other than English) will convey to the recipients useful information as to how willing researchers or project workers are to relate to participants in ways accessible to them. Leaflets should be written in consultation with the kind of young people at whom they are aimed, to avoid language which is patronising or confusing. Humour, where appropriate and possible, will be appreciated.

Of course, not every disabled child or young person will be able to read a leaflet or, if they can do so, necessarily be interested in or remember its contents. Nonetheless, information leaflets are a useful resource for disabled children and young people who might potentially be involved in a project, as are other media like audio and videotapes.

Preparation

Information leaflets for children and young people need to be brief. Researchers also need to produce, however, a fuller explanation of their proposed project, its different stages, the ethical issues arising at each and how these will be dealt with, in as clear and accessible form as possible. This may form part of the research proposal or be supplementary to it. Alderson (1995, Section 2) outlines in some detail the kinds of questions which should be addressed within such a document, including information on what will happen to people during the research, how data will be used, confidentiality, research methods and so on. She recommends that each project should have a user-friendly working title in words that anyone can easily understand (in addition to any formal title that is necessary). She also gives examples of the kinds of information that should be included to help children and young people decide whether they wish to participate and what the implications of agreeing or refusing might be. For disabled children and young people used to complying with the wishes of adults, reassurance that it is all right not to participate is vital. In the experience of The Who Cares? Trust, proper preparation and explanations before involvement make all the difference (Barbara Fletcher, personal communication).

Careful thought needs to be given to whether there is any possibility that children or young people may be distressed as a result of participation in interviews, perhaps because it may touch on an upsetting experience. What strategies are going to be adopted to minimise this possibility? What support will be offered if participants do become upset? What reassurances will project workers give to children and young people on confidentiality? What will happen if abuse or child protection becomes an issue?

(For more discussion on these issues see the National Children's Bureau *Guidelines for Research* and Mahon *et al.*, 1996. For more on support following interviews, see below.)

Approaches and techniques

Research or work with disabled children and young people should embody the same principles and procedures as good practice in research with adults. Thus, there needs to be careful attention to issues like location and timing of encounters, their length, introductions, rapport building, setting boundaries, giving respondents clear options not to answer certain questions and bringing any 'interview'[1] to a conclusion (see above for practical examples). With disabled children and young people who live away from their own families or spend much of their time in educational institutions, there will be additional issues in negotiating appropriate locations to meet. McCrum and Bernal (1994) provide a succinct and useful overview of many of the issues confronting researchers wishing to interview children; Beresford (1997) reviews additional issues to be confronted in research involving disabled children and young people. Her *Personal Accounts: Involving Disabled Children in Research* is a key resource, reviewing the literature on the relative merits of a wide variety of different research techniques involving disabled children and young people, both as individuals and in groups.

Opinions vary greatly on how structured interviews with children and young people should be, as Cavet (1995) points out. This will obviously depend partly on the subject matter of the research and partly on the age of the children concerned. Beresford's review (1997) provides useful hints on undertaking interviews as well as group discussions, observation and other approaches, including the use of drawing and written materials, visual analogues, play interviews and semi-projective techniques. Robina Shah (personal communication) recommends the use of simple pictures and symbols to tell a story in the research process, which may be especially useful with children whose spoken English is limited. Sensitivity and flexibility are clearly vital, as is building in sufficient time within the overall process for extensive piloting to be undertaken so that lessons learnt from early attempts can be incorporated subsequently.

The format of questions laid out within *The Memorandum of Good Practice in Video Recorded Interviews* (Home Office/Department of

---

[1] 'Interview' is used here to convey a consultation, meeting or encounter between researcher and disabled child or young person about their views or experiences. Since this may involve all kinds of interactions, the term 'interview' is used simply as shorthand.

Health, 1992), though devised for other purposes, may be of interest to some researchers, particularly the phrasing of open and closed questions. For non-speaking children, ideas on asking non-leading but facilitative questions are given in Marchant and Page (1993, 1997).

Mahon *et al.* (1996) raise a number of issues at the end of their article in relation to undertaking interviews with children – including ways in which any tendency for children to be 'suggestible' may be overcome; how their motivation may be maintained; considerations relating to privacy and location and the possibility of meeting away from parents or other family members; and questions about how data should be recorded. (In their experience, giving children control over a tape recorder was felt to aid not only their willingness to be taped but also the rapport between researcher and respondent.) Other points noted by them relate to the practicalities associated with making contact, failure to keep appointments (how far was this a form of refusal?) and the relative priority of the research, and its main focus, to other priorities within the family and for the child.

For the most part, research with disabled children and young people will be conducted by adults (though the report of Barnardo's Young Interviewers Project in Alderson, 1995, makes salutary reading). There will therefore be an inevitable imbalance of power between respondent and interviewer. McCrum and Bernal (1994) and Mahon *et al.* (1996) have suggestions for minimising this power imbalance through innovative research methods and the use of group interviews, etc. (See also Hazel, 1996, on 'Elicitation techniques with young people', though this does not address specific issues relating to impairment and disability.)

After the interview

There is, rightly, some concern within the literature about possible adverse consequences of the research on the children involved.

Most commentators advocate that researchers should consider the consequences of their work, give children the power to refuse consent to participate, and be enabled to terminate an interview at any point in the research process. The National Children's Bureau guidelines contain a paragraph on 'debriefing', which requires that those who have been interviewed should be encouraged to discuss their experience of the research so that unforeseen effects can be monitored.

They also suggest that researchers have a responsibility to assist participants, where necessary, in receiving appropriate help or counselling where painful or difficult experiences have been explored. Where children may experience distress following an interview – for example, because it has touched on a painful topic or an upsetting experience – researchers on Foundation-funded projects will be expected to ensure that further help or counselling is offered to that child or young person from an appropriate source if this is what the child wishes, and is costed into the project budget. In the experience of The Who Cares? Trust, such support may need to be provided sporadically and informally over time. If it is feasible, having someone to ring is important. Peer support is also a possibility. Might funding be used to facilitate a group meeting at regular intervals so young people (and project staff) can keep in touch? (Barbara Fletcher, personal communication). Where disclosures of abuse are a possibility, steps and strategies need to be worked out in advance to deal with the eventuality (National Children's Bureau, 1993; Mahon et al., 1996).

Researchers also need to be sensitive to the possibility of black and ethnic minority children disclosing experiences of racism; they may feel unable to contribute fully to the interview or project until this has been addressed.

In moving to close an interview, it is important that children know in advance that it is drawing towards the end so that they are able to get their thoughts and feelings together and say anything which they have left to say. McCrum and Bernal (1994) stress that it is

important to ask children if there is anything they have said that they now wish not to be published, broadcast or otherwise included in outputs from the research in any form. They too advocate asking children at the end what they felt about the interview and how it could have been made better for them.

Payment

The National Children's Bureau guidelines suggest that it is appropriate to compensate children and young people who have participated in projects for their time and effort. The traditional practice has been that this payment should be in kind (usually a gift voucher) and that it would normally be given at the end of an interview and thus not offered as an inducement to participate. In the study of the impact of the Child Support Act on children a payment in cash was made, although again this was not mentioned in advance when negotiating the child's consent to the interview (Mahon *et al.*, 1996). The costs of such payments or fees should be included in research project budgets at the outset.

Feedback to children

There is a welcome, and growing, trend towards feeding back to research participants the outcomes of the projects in which they have taken part. Where disabled children and young people have been involved in projects supported by the Foundation, the expectation is that key, relevant findings from the project will be fed back to them in appropriate formats, whether this is in illustrated leaflet or cartoon form, via audio or videotapes, through leaflets or by other means, including individual or group visits or meetings.

4 Equal opportunities for participation

Different research and development projects will be interested in the views and experiences of different disabled children and young people. The Foundation is concerned to ensure that as wide a spread as possible of disabled children and young people of different ages, genders, backgrounds, ethnic groups and with different impairments should be included in projects and welcomes innovative approaches for their inclusion. Disabled children and young people are clearly very diverse in all kinds of ways, including their age, developmental maturity and verbal skills. Duly respecting this diversity means adapting project procedures and methods appropriately. There is a small, but growing, body of experience in this area.

Age

Cavet (1995) looks briefly at issues of age in relation to interviewing children and young people and the different methodologies which need to be employed. Beresford (1997) reviews ways in which interviews with children will need to be adapted to take account of their age and level of communicative ability.

Gender

Mahon *et al.* (1996) report that their less successful interviews were those conducted with boys; they speculate that interviews using a male researcher would have been beneficial. Clearly, the same issues arise in relation to the use of same sex interviewers with children and young people as they do with adults, particularly where the subject matter is of a personal kind.

Involving children from black and minority ethnic groups

It is important that disabled children and young people from black and minority ethnic groups are included within research and development projects. This may involve the employment of a researcher/consultant from an appropriate ethnic minority background. This may facilitate the child's involvement in the project; it may also ensure that the interview is appropriately conducted in respect of language, culture and other issues. Researchers who are not themselves from a black or minority ethnic background are often hesitant about how to involve people from black and minority ethnic groups in their projects. They are anxious that as they are not black themselves, they will 'do something wrong'. But researchers or project workers can develop the necessary skills, knowledge and sensitivity to work appropriately in this area and/or build time and resources into their projects to work in partnership with black and minority ethnic organisations and individuals with the relevant expertise and networks.

Some children and families from black and ethnic minority groups may be more expressive in a mother tongue other than English; this option needs to be offered to them. If the research or project workers are not themselves bilingual or multilingual, this will require collaborative working with a researcher or interviewer with appropriate language and other skills and/or careful working with a trained interpreter who speaks the relevant mother tongue. Working successfully with interpreters demands attention to a whole range of issues. Robina Shah (1995) gives helpful advice in her publication *The Silent Minority* (see especially pp. 54–9). This is vital reading for anyone contemplating working with interpreters. McCrum and Bernal (1994) also have useful advice on working with translators and interpreters when interviewing children in their pamphlet. Clearly, information leaflets aimed at children and young people who may participate in projects need to be made available in relevant community languages and appropriately illustrated. Projects also need to think about how they will get their messages and findings across to audiences from a variety of black and minority ethnic groups. Audio and videotapes and leaflets in relevant community languages may need to be prepared – and disseminated – via a range of community organisations, groups and facilities and the black and ethnic minority media. Consult with appropriate organisations or individuals in your area or your local race equality council for help and advice.

The Foundation is anxious to ensure that the needs of black and ethnic minority people are adequately reflected in its Social Care and Disability Programme; it is likely that guidance on working with interpreters and doing research with black and ethnic minority families will soon be made available.

Children with sensory, profound or multiple impairments

Involving children with different impairments will require a range of skills and approaches. Pat Fitton's book *Listen to Me* (1994) provides many useful ideas on listening to children and young people with profound and multiple impairments. In particular, questionnaires for children with visual impairments, deaf children or children with learning difficulties will need to be creatively designed and may need to be differently presented from questionnaires aimed at other groups of children. As Ruth Marchant points out, it is as dangerous to automatically assume certain children cannot participate via certain methods as it is to assume unquestioningly that they can. Either/or, yes/no and multiple choice questions can all work well for children with sensory or learning difficulties (Ruth Marchant, personal communication).

It is important that projects should make every attempt to include children with whom it is not straightforward to communicate through conventional printed or spoken means. Growing expertise does exist in these areas; prospective researchers should build into their proposals time, space and money for them to consult with or employ other researchers with appropriate skills and experience or to become more adept in these areas themselves. (For insights about researching within the deaf community, see Jones and Pullen, 1992, and Jones, 1995).

The choice of interpreters, communicators or facilitators, where they are needed to facilitate the child's communication and involvement in the research process, is crucial. The use of individuals who usually play one particular role in a child's life (e.g. a teacher) may have a strong effect on the responses children make to particular questions and may, therefore, need to be avoided. So far as possible the young person needs to be given a choice, perhaps a guided or limited one. The organisation or carer with whom the young person is involved (e.g. school, parent, social worker) could be asked to suggest three possible facilitators who are familiar with the child's communication, and available, and the young person could choose one of the three. (An open choice might pose other difficulties.)

The NSPCC, in its work on disclosure interviews with disabled children who may have been sexually abused, has developed helpful strategies which have a wider relevance to research projects involving children with multiple impairments. It has found that to facilitate the child in communicating, it is necessary to make available a person with whom the child is familiar, who can interpret for them, as well as the person with expertise in the type of interview being undertaken: that is, a combination of the skills of the child's communicator with those of the interviewer is vital (see Marchant and Page, 1993).

Until recently, there has been little written material available on ways of including disabled children and young people with different impairments in research projects. Bryony Beresford's review of the literature on methodology in this area is a useful resource for prospective researchers (Beresford, 1997). Imaginative researchers should also be able to adapt methods followed successfully in research with disabled adults with different impairments (for example adults with learning difficulties – see Ward, 1997; deaf adults – see Jones, 1995) to projects concerning disabled children and young people with similar impairments. The involvement of interviewers with similar impairments as those they are interviewing will be an advantage in some projects either because this aids communication (as with researcher and interviewee both using British Sign Language) or because of ease of rapport. As one of the young interviewers in the Barnardo's project said:

> The boy I talked to was brain damaged, and he kept jumping around and on and off the bench but he still kept talking and I think it was a good interview. It didn't matter because I am only 16, whereas if I had been an adult I think I would have had to make him behave more quietly, and I don't think he would have told me so much then. (Alderson, 1995)

5 Moving on

Appropriately involving disabled children and young people in research and development projects poses many ethical, methodological and logistical challenges. Much remains to be done. Over the next few years we hope to continue to distil and disseminate ideas for better practice coming from disabled children and young people, Joseph Rowntree Foundation-funded projects and from elsewhere, via further publications, guidelines and workshops as appropriate.

If you wish to be kept informed of these or if you have ideas and examples of innovative developments to share, contact:

Dr Linda Ward
Programme Adviser (Disability)
Joseph Rowntree Foundation
c/o Norah Fry Research Centre
University of Bristol
3 Priory Road
Bristol
BS8 1TX

6 Checklist for action

In planning your project, check that you have considered all the following aspects of involving disabled children and young people within it.

1. Involvement throughout

■ Have you involved disabled children or young people wherever possible *throughout* the project:
   – as partners (in planning and managing the project)?
   – as consultants or advisers?
   – as interviewers, researchers or project workers?
   – as disseminators or workshop speakers?
   – in other ways?

2. Ethics and consent

■ Have you considered and addressed all the ethical issues involved in your project?

■ Have you thought through carefully how you will get informed consent from the children and young people involved?

■ Have you built in checks so that participating children can discontinue their involvement whenever they wish?

■ Have you planned how you can show them how they can do this?

3. Preparation and support

■ Have you paid attention to the need for participating children to have:
 – proper preparation and information for their involvement?
 – support during and afterwards as necessary?

4. Methodology

■ Have you carefully reviewed alternative methodologies and their strengths, weaknesses and appropriateness for:
 – the purpose of your particular project?
 – the nature of the impairments of the children and young people concerned?
 – their age and circumstances, etc.?

5. Practical issues

■ Have you paid attention to the practicalities of involving disabled children and young people in all aspects of your project?

■ Have you thought through how their different needs can best be met?

6. Including all children

■ Have you assumed some children (perhaps those with multiple or profound impairments, communication difficulties or challenging behaviour) cannot be included within your project? Are you right? What steps could you take to include them?

■ Are you attempting to include children across ages, impairments, genders, backgrounds and ethnic groups, as appropriate to the project? Have you reviewed appropriate strategies and approaches for doing so?

7. Dissemination and feedback

■ Have you thought through how findings from your project can be fed back to disabled children and young people, in ways that are accessible and interesting to them?

■ Do you need to translate key messages from your project into British Sign Language or other community languages?

■ What networks, organisations or community groups would be useful channels for dissemination?

8. Costs and budget

■ Have you costed in the expenses entailed in all the above:
  – extra time for preparation?
  – resources for information leaflets?
  – costs for facilitation?
  – fees and expenses for participation, transport and venues?
  – possible support costs, during and after the project?
  – feedback and dissemination costs?

9. Proposal

■ Does your project proposal or plan detail the steps you have taken on all the above?

■ Have you outlined any additional safeguards and steps you are proposing within your project to ensure that the involvement of disabled children and young people is as positive for them as possible?

10. Value and partnership

■ Are you sure your project is necessary and worthwhile? Does it have the potential to bring about positive changes for disabled children and young people and their families?

■ Have you consulted with disabled children and young people (or their representatives) to see what they think of your ideas? Have you taken note of their views and amended your proposal to take account of them?

■ Have you built partnership with relevant disabled people's, young people's or ethnic minority organisations into your project to make it stronger?

References

(* Essential reading)

*Alderson, P. (1995) *Listening to Children: Children, Ethics and Social Research*. Barkingside: Barnardo's

Alderson, P. and Goodey, C. (1996) 'Research with disabled children: how useful is child-centred ethics?', *Children and Society*, Vol. 10, No. 2, pp. 106–16

Ash, A., Bellew, J., Davies, M., Newman, T. and Richardson, L. (1996) *Everybody In? The Experience of Disabled Students in Colleges of Further Education*. Barkingside: Barnardo's

*Beresford, B. (1997) *Personal Accounts: Involving Disabled Children in Research*. London: The Stationery Office

Blackburn, M. (1994) 'Experiences of disability associations: Association for Spina Bifida and/or Hydrocephalus', in *Collecting Information on Disability: Ethical and Legal Issues*. London: SCOPE

Cavet, J. (1995) *Interviewing Children and Young People with Chronic Health Conditions: Some Issues for Researchers* (unpublished). Available from Judith Cavet, School of Social Sciences, Staffordshire University, College Road, Stoke-on-Trent, ST4 2DG

Children and Society (1996) Vol. 10, No. 2 (Issue focusing on the ethics and methodology of research with children)

Department for Education and Welsh Office (1994) *Code of Practice on the Identification and Assessment of Special Educational Needs*. London: HMSO

Department of Health (1996) *Patient's Charter on Services for Children and Young People*. London: HMSO

Disability, Handicap and Society (1992) Vol. 7, No. 2: Special issue, 'Researching Disability'

Fitton, P. (1994) *Listen to Me: Communicating the Needs of People with Profound Intellectual and Multiple Disabilities*. London: Jessica Kingsley

Hazel, N. (1996) 'Elicitation techniques with young people', *Social Research Update*, 12, Spring. Guildford: University of Surrey, Department of Sociology

Home Office/Department of Health (1992) *The Memorandum of Good Practice in Video Recorded Interviews of Child Witnesses for Criminal Proceedings*. London: HMSO

Jones, L. (1995) *Doing Deaf Research* (video). York: University of York, Social Policy Research Unit

Jones, L. and Pullen, G. (1992) 'Cultural differences: deaf and hearing researchers working together', *Disability, Handicap and Society*, Vol. 7, No. 2, pp. 189–96

Lansdown, G. (1995) *Taking Part: Children's Participation in Decision Making*. London: Institute for Public Policy Research

Mahon, A., Glendinning, C., Clarke, K. and Craig, G. (1996) 'Researching children: methods and ethics', *Children and Society*, Vol. 10, No. 2, pp. 145–54

Marchant, R. and Page, M. (1993) *Bridging the Gap: Child Protection Work with Children with Multiple Disabilities*. London: NSPCC

Marchant, R. and Page, M. (1997) 'Interviewing disabled children', in J. Jones, and H. Westcott (eds) *Memorandum on the Memorandum*. London: Arena

McCrum, S. and Bernal, P. (1994) *Interviewing Children: A Training Pack for Journalists.* Buckfastleigh: Children's Voices

Minkes, J., Robinson, C. and Weston, C. (1994) 'Consulting with children: interviews with children using residential respite care services', *Disability and Society*, Vol. 9, No. 1, pp. 47–57

Morris, J. (1996) *Encouraging User Involvement in Commissioning: A Resource for Commissioners.* London: Department of Health

Morrow, V. and Richards, M. (1996) 'The ethics of social research with children: an overview', *Children and Society*, Vol. 10, No. 2, pp. 90–105

National Children's Bureau (1993) *Guidelines for Research.* London: NCB

Oakley, A. (1991) 'Interviewing women: a contradiction in terms', in H. Roberts (ed.) *Doing Feminist Research.* London: Routledge

Oliver, M. (1992) 'Changing the social relations of research production?', *Disability, Handicap and Society*, Vol. 7, No. 2, pp. 101–14

Roberts, H. (1991) *Doing Feminist Research.* London: Routledge

Russell, P. (1996) 'Listening to children with special educational needs', in R. Davie and D. Galloway (eds) *Listening to Children in Education.* London: David Fulton

Shah, R. (1995) *The Silent Minority: Children with Disabilities in Asian Families.* London: National Children's Bureau

The Who Cares? Trust (1993) *Code of Practice for Media Representatives and Young People Under 18 In or Ex-care.* London: The Who Cares? Trust

Townsley, R. and Gyde, K. (1997a) *Plain Facts: Information about Research for People with Learning Difficulties*. Bristol: University of Bristol, Norah Fry Research Centre

Townsley, R. and Gyde, K. (1997b) *Writing Plain Facts*. York: Joseph Rowntree Foundation

Tozer, R. and Thornton, P. (1995) *A Meeting of Minds: Older People as Research Advisers*. York: University of York, Social Policy Research Unit

United Nations (1983) Convention on the Rights of the Child

Ward, L. (1997) 'Practising partnership: involving people with intellectual disabilities in research', in M. Bach and M. Rioux (eds) *Disability Discourse: Research, Public Policy and Human Rights*. North York, Ontario: Roeher Institute (in press)

Ward, L. and Flynn, M. (1994) 'What matters most: disability, research and empowerment', in M. Rioux and M. Bach (eds) *Disability is Not Measles: New Research Paradigms in Disability*. North York, Ontario: Roeher Institute

Organisations

Barnardo's, Tanners Lane, Barkingside, Ilford, Essex IG6 1QG
Tel: 0181 550 8822

Children's Voices, 23 Silver Street, Buckfastleigh, Devon
TQ11 0BQ
Tel: 01364 642787

Institute for Public Policy Research, 30–32 Southampton Street,
London WC2E 7RA
Tel: 0171 379 9400

**National Children's Bureau (and Council for Disabled
Children)**, 8 Wakley Street, Islington, London EC1V 7QE
Tel: 0171 843 6000

Norah Fry Research Centre, University of Bristol, 3 Priory Road,
Bristol, BS8 1TX
Tel: 0117 923 8137

Social Policy Research Unit, University of York, Heslington, York
YO1 5DD
Tel: 01904 433608

The Who Cares? Trust, Kemp House, 152–160 City Road,
London EC1V 2NP
Tel: 0171 251 3117